CHARLIE PUTH   VOICENOTES

ISBN 978-1-5400-3290-4

HAL•LEONARD®

Visit Hal Leonard Online at
www.halleonard.com

Contact us:
Hal Leonard
7777 West Bluemound Road
Milwaukee, WI 53213
Email: info@halleonard.com

In Europe, contact:
Hal Leonard Europe Limited
42 Wigmore Street
Marylebone, London, W1U 2RN
Email: info@halleonardeurope.com

In Australia, contact:
Hal Leonard Australia Pty. Ltd.
4 Lentara Court
Cheltenham, Victoria, 3192 Australia
Email: info@halleonard.com.au

THE WAY I AM

Words and Music by CHARLIE PUTH
and JACOB KASHER HINDLIN

Recorded a half step lower.

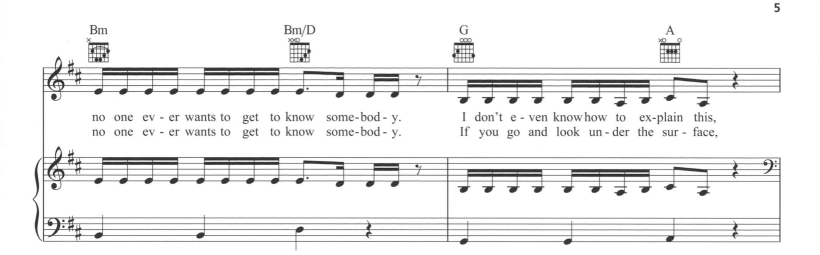

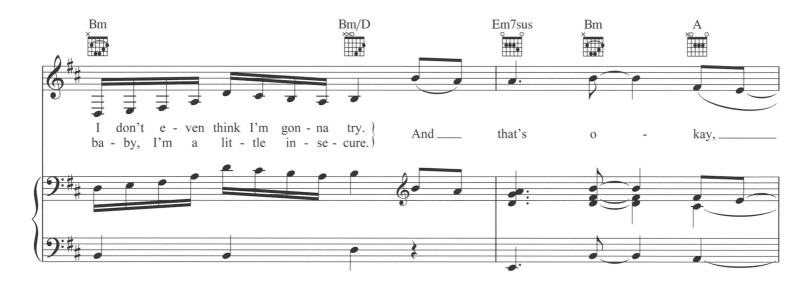

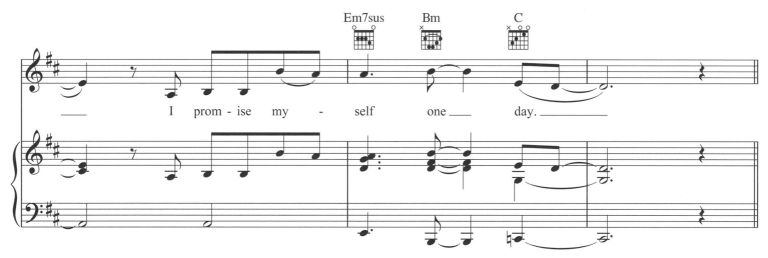

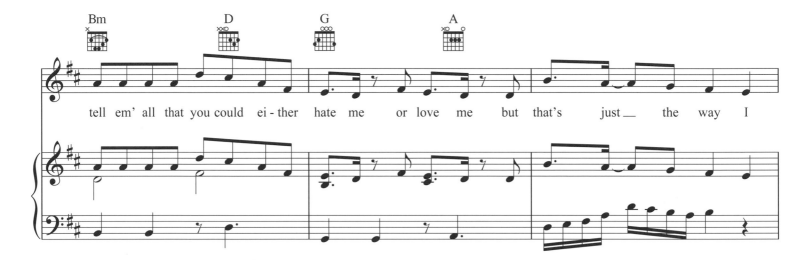

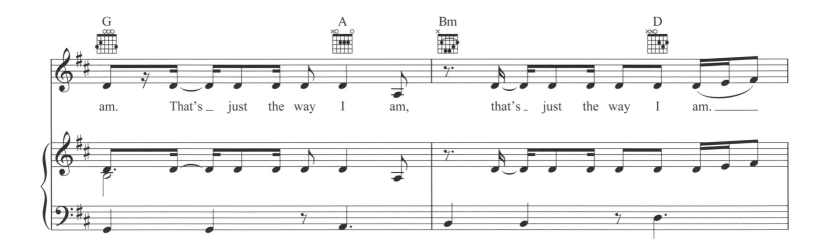

that's just ___ the way I...   I'm-ma tell em' all, _____ I'm-ma
                                That's just the way I am,

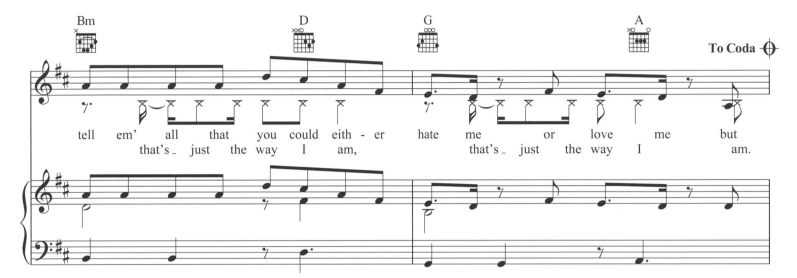

tell em' all that you could eith-er   hate me   or   love   me   but
that's _ just the way I am,   that's _ just the way I   am.

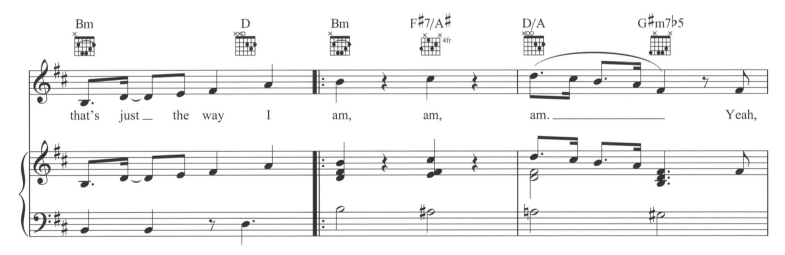

that's just ___ the way I   am,   am,   am. _____   Yeah,

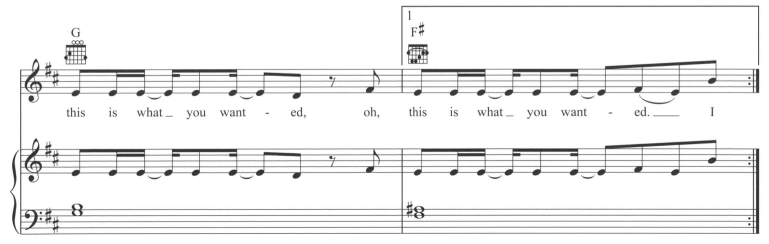

this is what _ you want - ed,   oh,   this is what _ you want - ed. ___   I

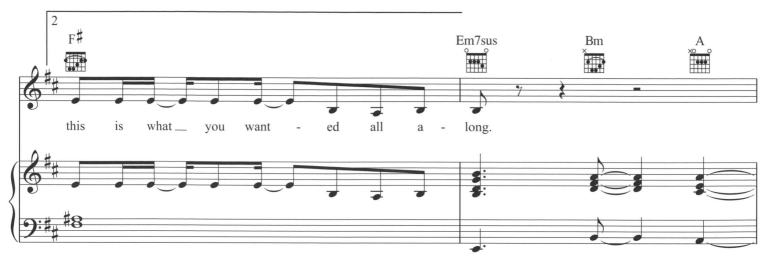

this is what __ you want - ed all a - long.

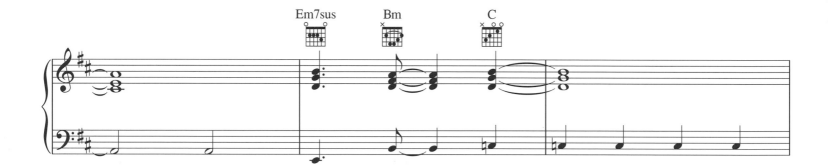

Ev-'ry-bod-y's try-ing to be fa-mous and I'm just try'n' to find a place to hide.

D.S. al Coda

CODA

that's just __ the way I am.

ATTENTION

Words and Music by CHARLIE PUTH
and JACOB KASHER HINDLIN

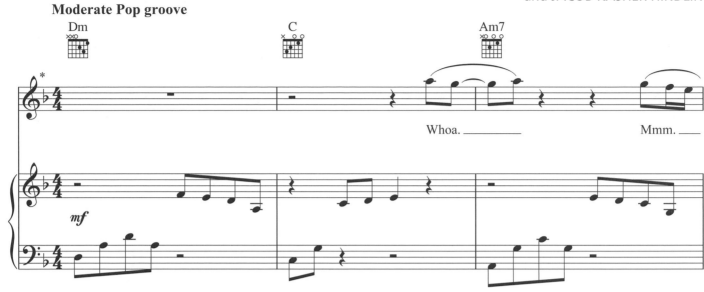

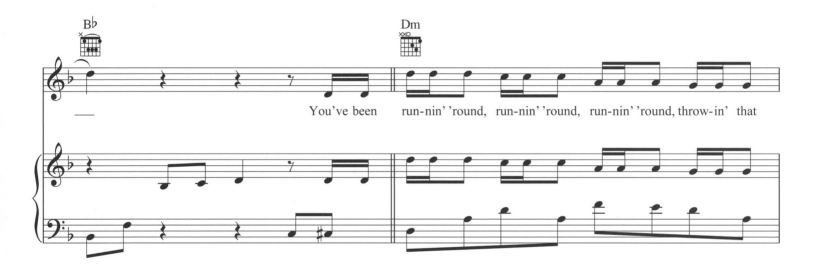

* Recorded a half step higher.

up. ____ You've been go-in' 'round, go-in' 'round, go-in' 'round ev-er-y

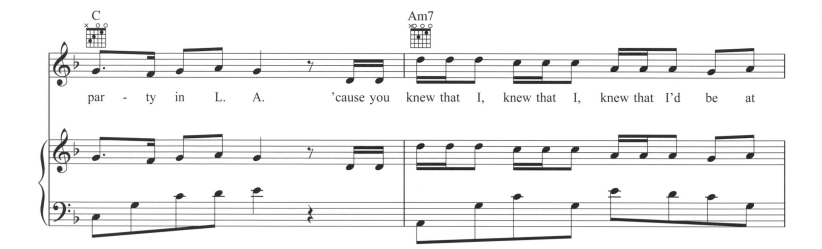

par-ty in L. A. 'cause you knew that I, knew that I, knew that I'd be at

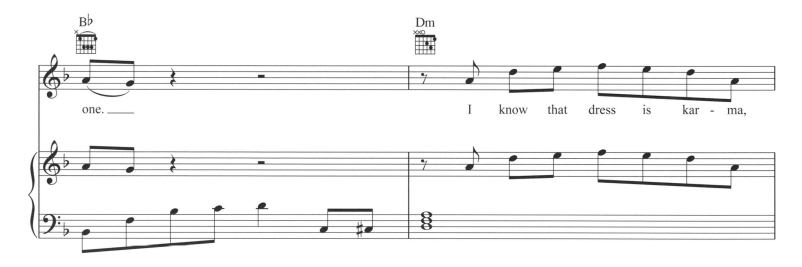

one. ____ I know that dress is kar-ma,

per-fume re-gret. You got me think-in' 'bout __ when you __ were mine. __

Ooh. _____ And now I'm all up on you; what you ex-pect? But

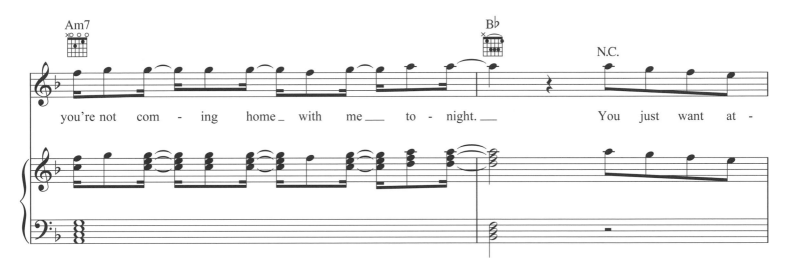

you're not com - ing home with me to - night. _____ You just want at -

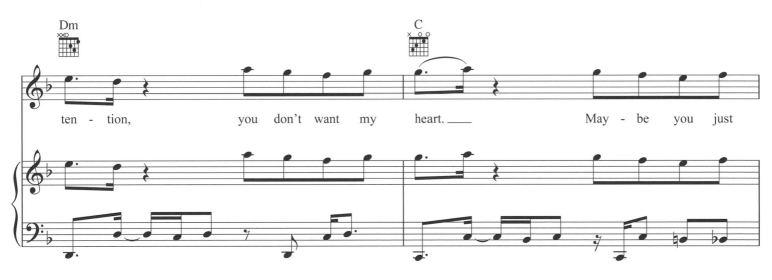

ten - tion, you don't want my heart. _____ May - be you just

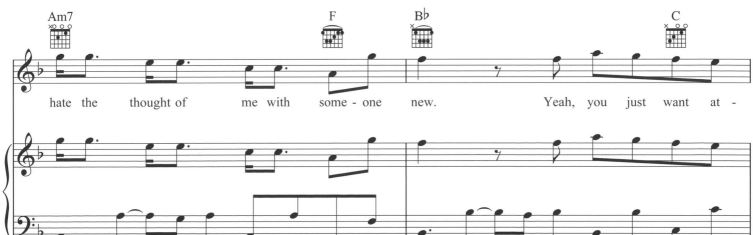

hate the thought of me with some - one new. Yeah, you just want at -

12

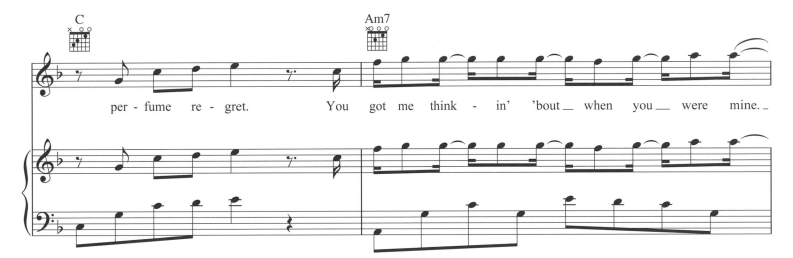

LA GIRLS

Words and Music by CHARLIE PUTH,
JACOB KASHER HINDLIN, SEAN DOUGLAS
and JASON EVIGAN

* *Recorded a half step higher.*

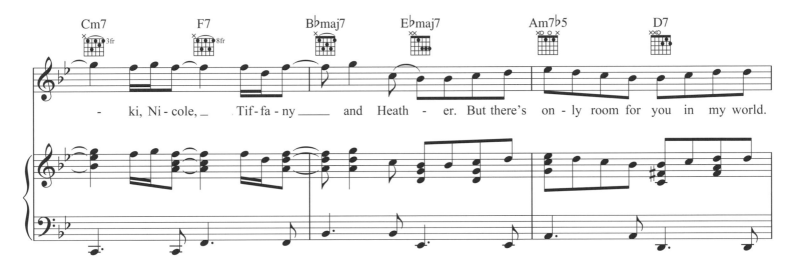

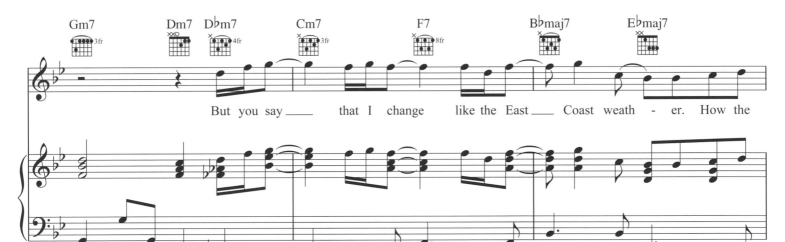

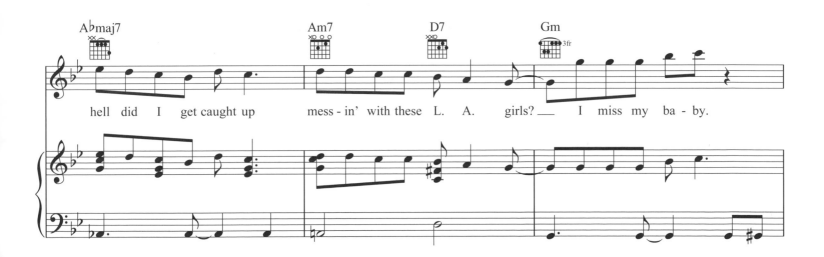

BOY

Words and Music by CHARLIE PUTH
and JACOB KASHER HINDLIN

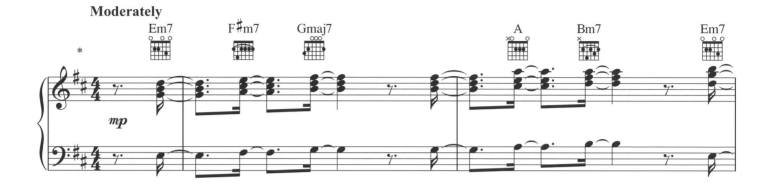

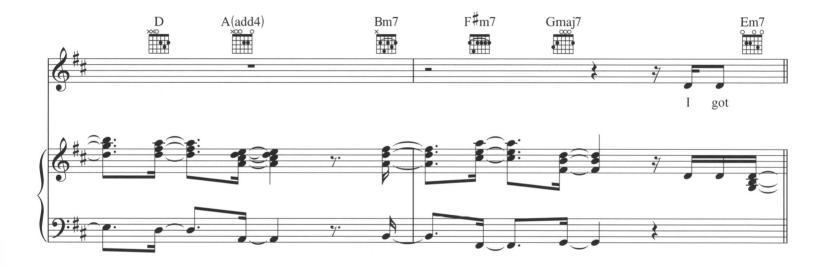

these girls try-'na lock me down and I al-ways up and leave. _ But for the
you need-ed a per-fect guy that-'ll make your par-ents proud. _ Guess you

*Recorded a half step lower.

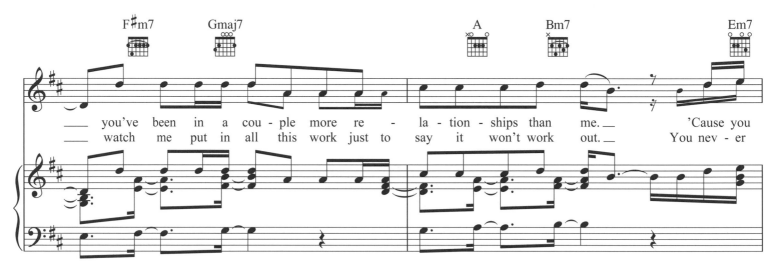

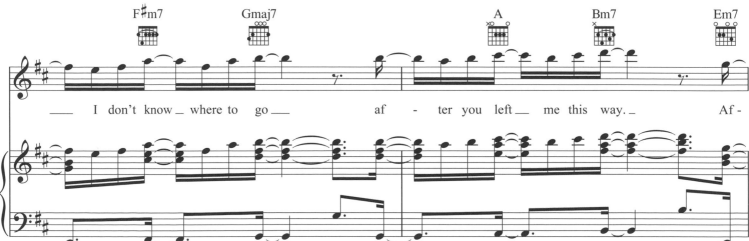

- ter you love me so good, how are you gon-na tell me you don't wan-na stay?

You tell me I'm too young, but I gave you what you want-ed.

Ba-by, how dare you treat me just like, like a

boy. You won't wake up be-side me 'cause I was born in the nine-ties.

Don't treat me like, boy, _____ ooh. _____

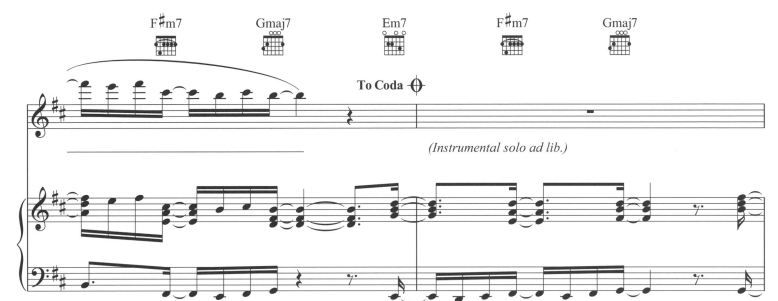

To Coda ⊕

(Instrumental solo ad lib.)

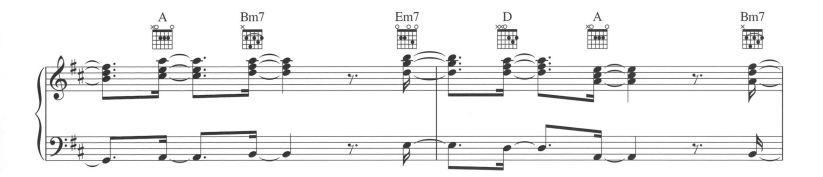

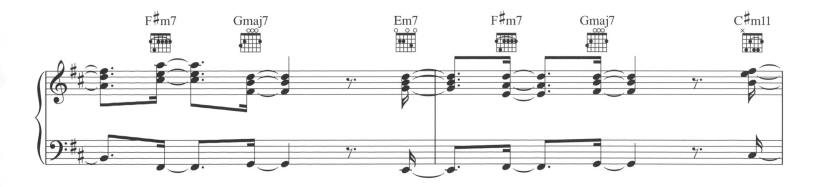

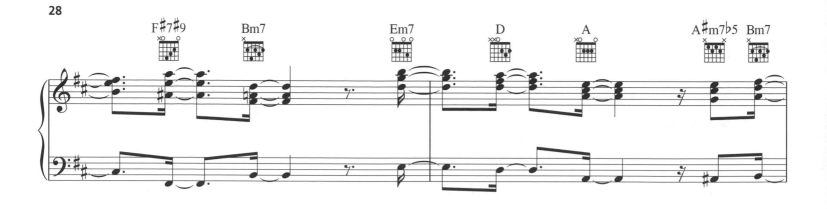

D.S. al Coda
(take 2nd ending)

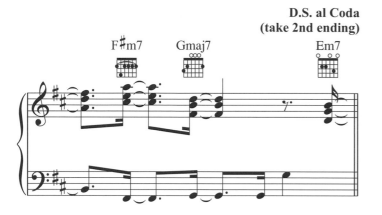

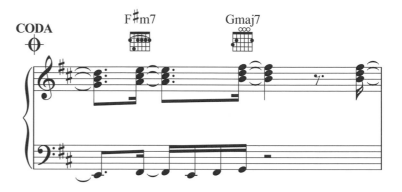

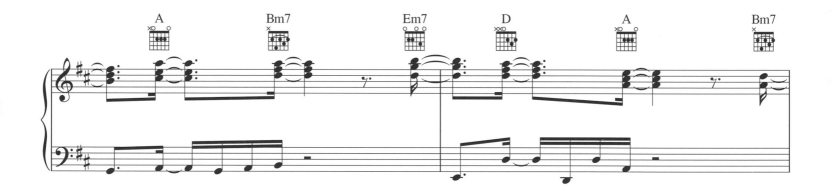

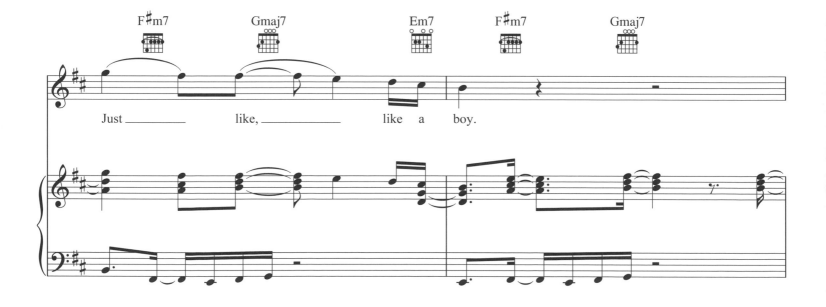

Just _____ like, _____ like a boy.

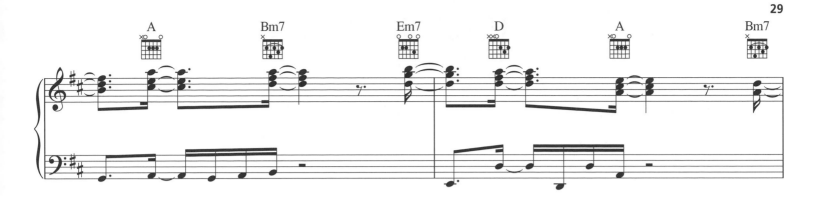

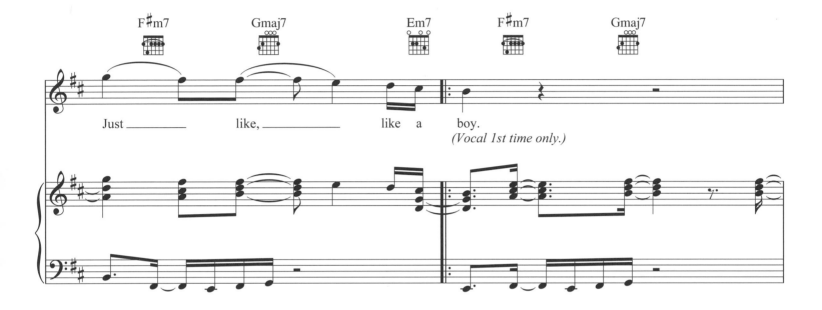

Just _____ like, _____ like a boy.
(Vocal 1st time only.)

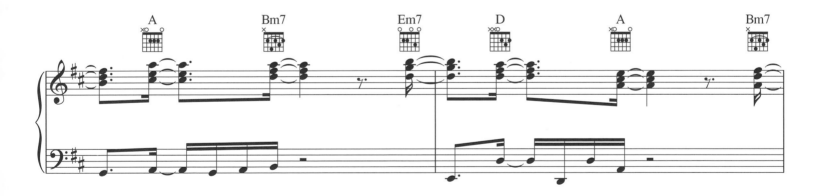

Repeat and Fade | **Optional Ending**

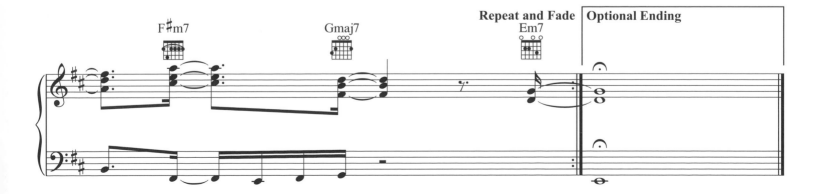

HOW LONG

Words and Music by CHARLIE PUTH,
JACOB KASHER HINDLIN and JUSTIN FRANKS

Moderate groove

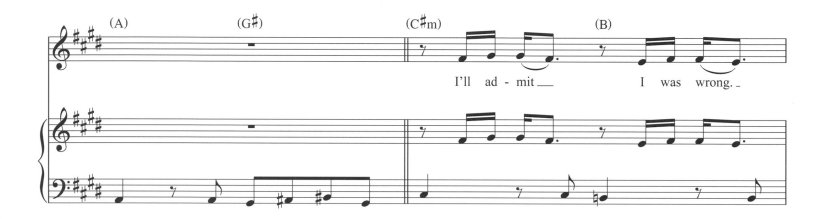

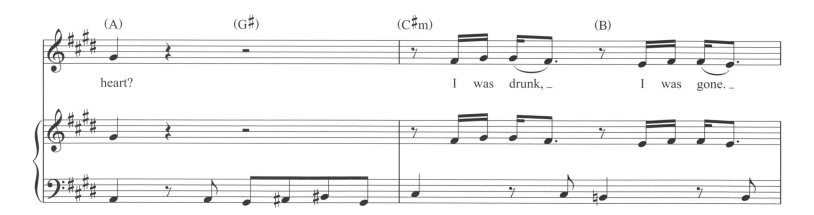

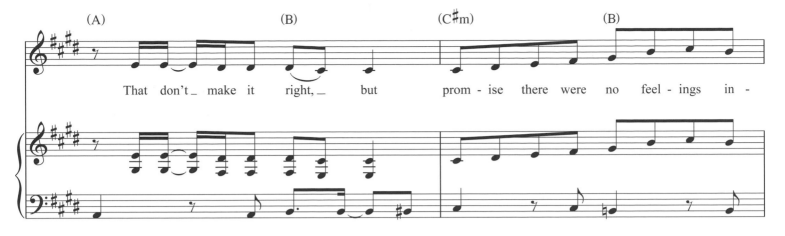

That don't_ make it right,_ but prom - ise there were no feel - ings in -

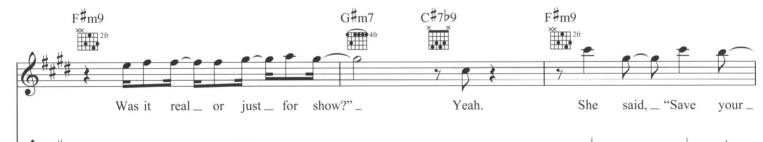

volved. She said,_ "Boy, tell ____ me hon - est - ly.

Was it real_ or just_ for show?"_ Yeah. She said,_ "Save your_

___ a - pol - o - gies. Ba - by, I __ just got - ta know. _ How _____

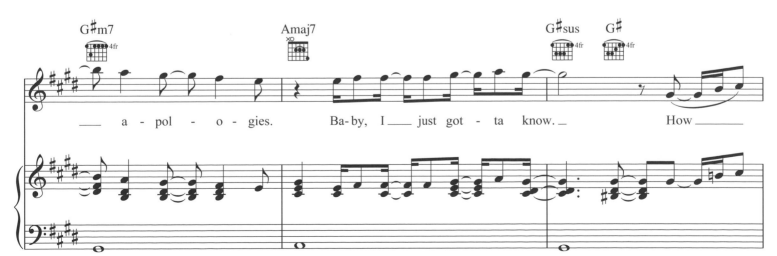

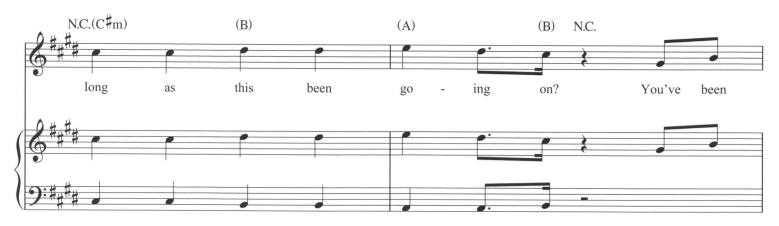

N.C.(C#m)   (B)   (A)   (B) N.C.

long as this been go - ing on? You've been

(C#m)   (B)   (A)   (G#)

creep-ing 'round on me while you're call-ing me ba - by. How _____

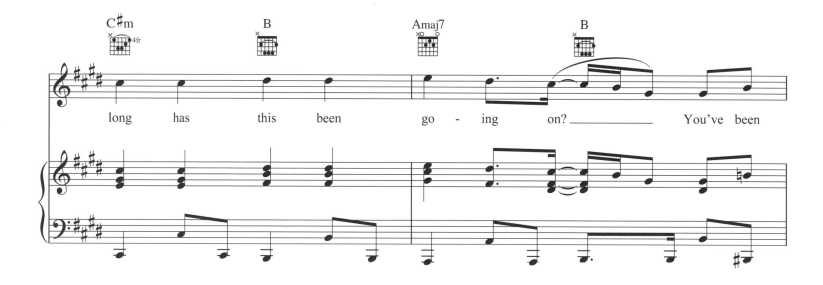

C#m   B   Amaj7   B

long has this been go - ing on? _____ You've been

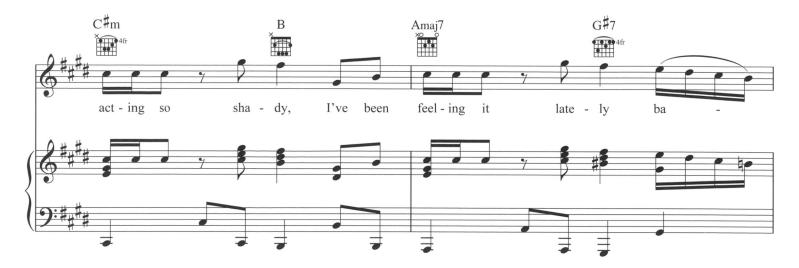

C#m   B   Amaj7   G#7

act-ing so sha-dy, I've been feel-ing it late-ly ba -

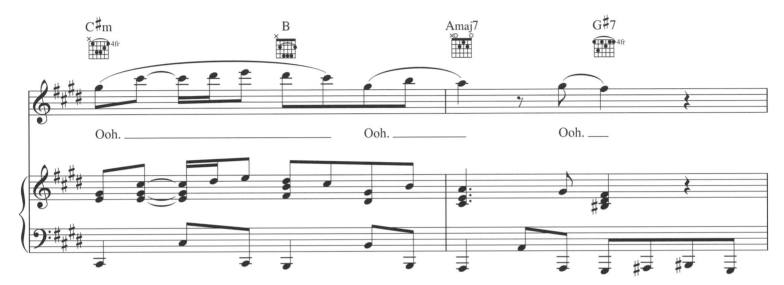

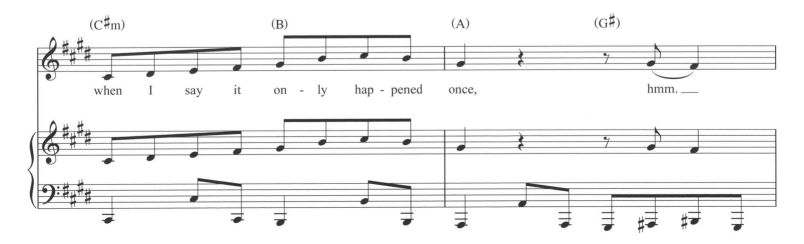

Ooh. _____ Ooh. _____ Ooh. _ She said, _ "Boy, tell _

____ me hon - est - ly. Was it real ___ or just ___ for show?" _

____ Yeah. _____ She said, _ "Save your ___ a - pol - o - gies.

Ba - by, I ___ just got - ta know. _ How _____

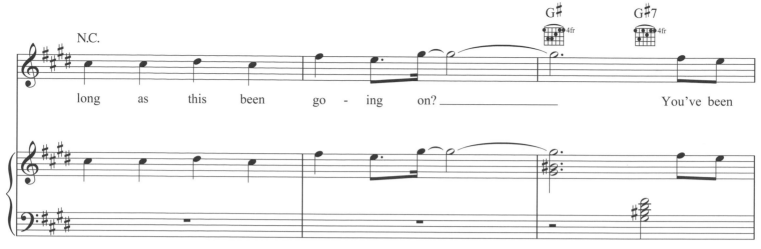

long as this been go - ing on? _____ You've been

creep-ing 'round on me while you're call-ing me ba - by. How _____

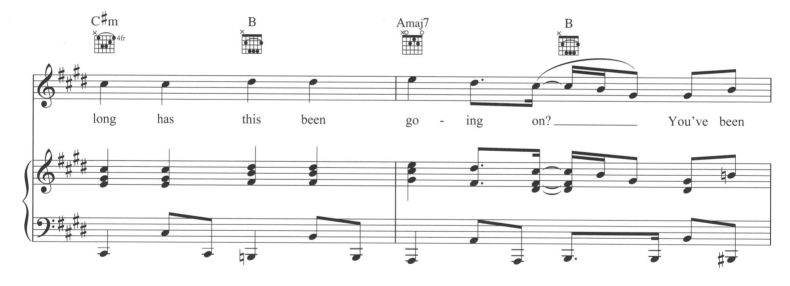

long has this been go - ing on? _____ You've been

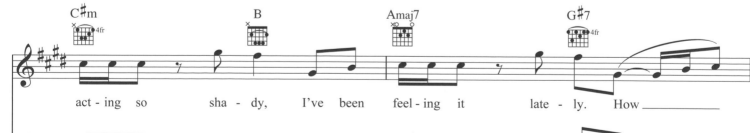

act-ing so sha - dy, I've been feel-ing it late - ly. How _____

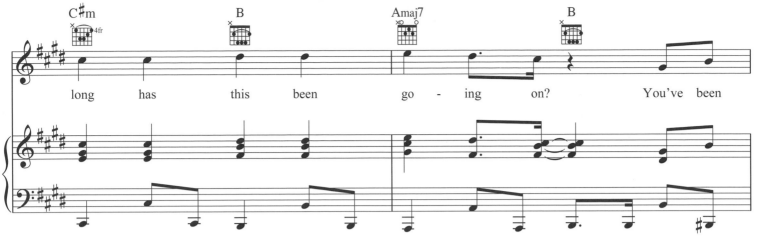

long has this been go-ing on? You've been

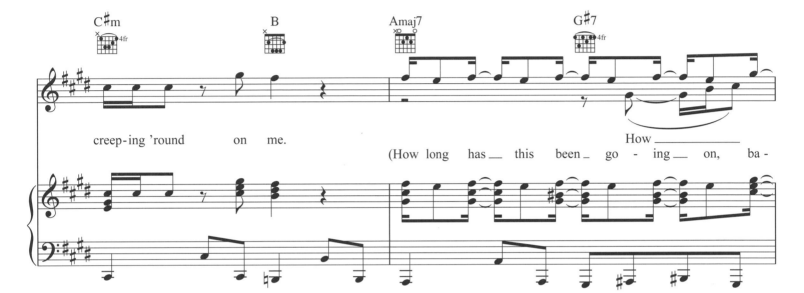

creep-ing 'round on me.

(How long has this been go-ing on, ba- How

long has this been go-ing on? You've been act-ing so sha-dy, I've been
-by?)

feel-ing it late-ly, ba- by."

DONE FOR ME

Words and Music by CHARLIE PUTH,
JACOB KASHER HINDLIN and JOHN HENRY RYAN

PATIENT

Words and Music by CHARLIE PUTH,
JACOB KASHER HINDLIN, BEN JOHNSON
and FRASER CHURCHILL

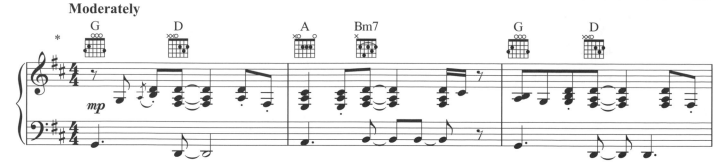

These mis - takes, I've made my fair share. _ When you

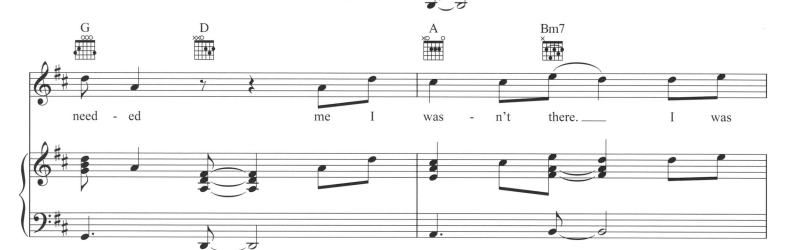

need - ed me I was - n't there. _ I was

young, I was dumb, I was so im-ma-ture. _ And the things that I did made you so in-se-cure. _ But

Recorded a half step lower.

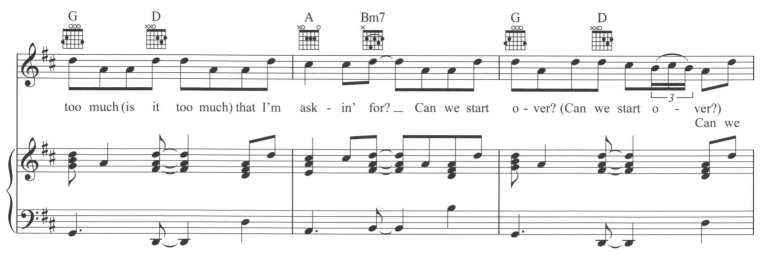

too much (is it too much) that I'm ask-in' for? ___ Can we start o-ver? (Can we start o-ver?) Can we

end this war? ___ I've been tak-in' your love, I've been wast-in' your time. ___ But is

there still a chance of me chang-in' your mind ___ be-fore you go walk-in'

out the door? ___ Oh, you ___ know I'm ___ not per-fect. If you ___

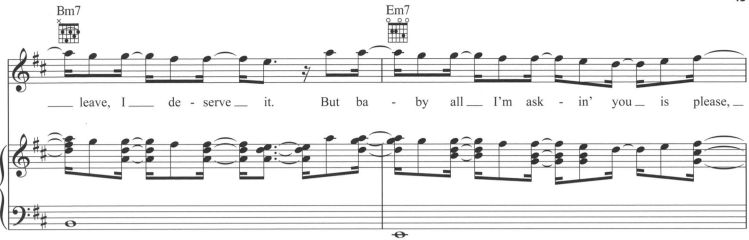

leave, I __ de - serve __ it. But ba - by all __ I'm ask - in' you __ is please, __

__ please. Oh, please _____ be _____ pa - tient with me. __

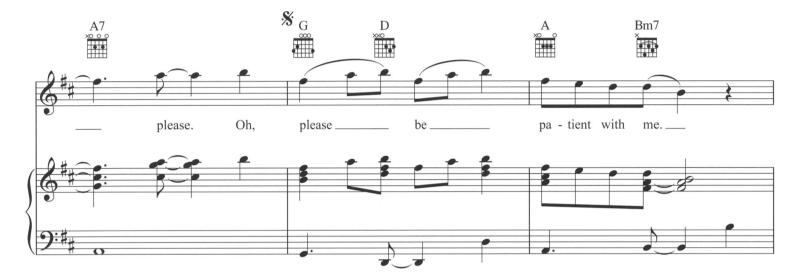

Please _____ be _____ pa - tient with me. _____ I know I'm not what you need _____ but

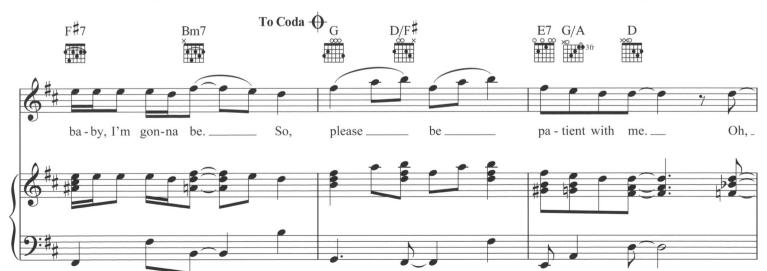

ba - by, I'm gon - na be. _____ So, please _____ be _____ pa - tient with me. __ Oh, __

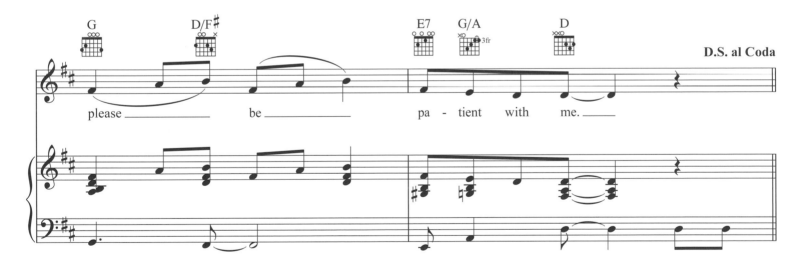

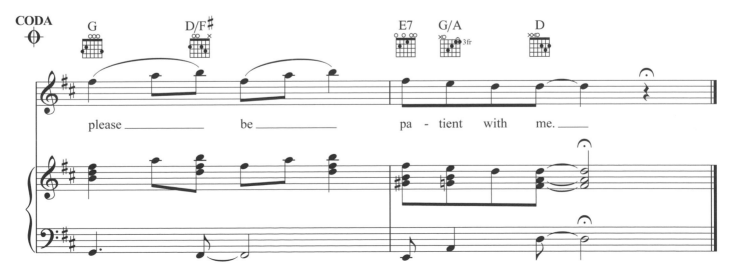

IF YOU LEAVE ME NOW

Words and Music by CHARLIE PUTH,
TOBIAS JESSO JR. and ROBIN LEE WILEY

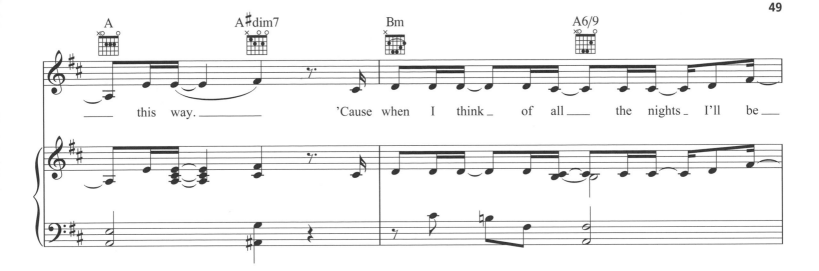

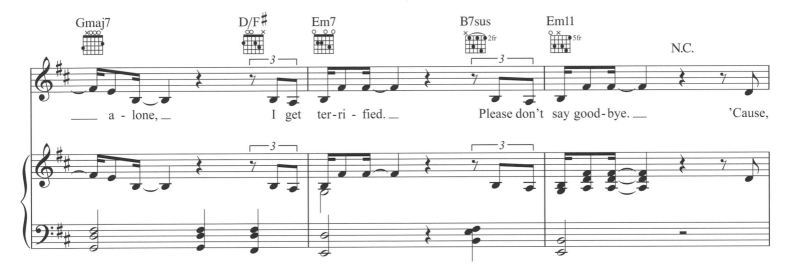

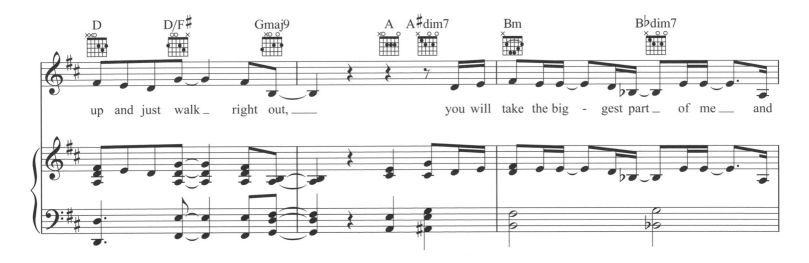

all the things___ that I___ be - lieve,___ ba - by, if you leave me___ now.___

When___ did we lose our way?___

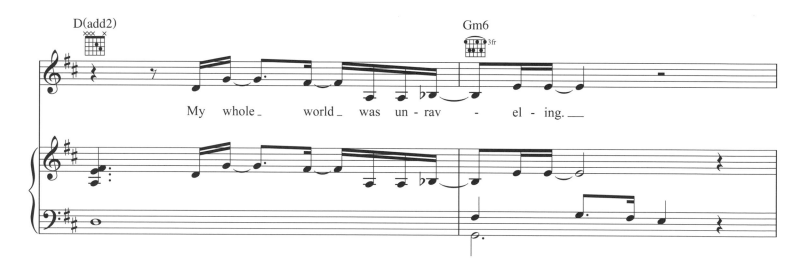

My whole___ world___ was un - rav - el - ing.___

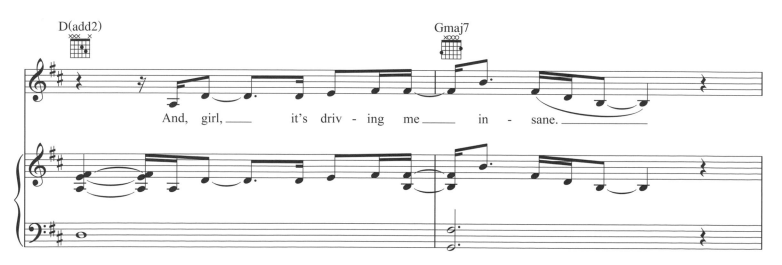

And, girl,___ it's driv - ing me___ in - sane.___

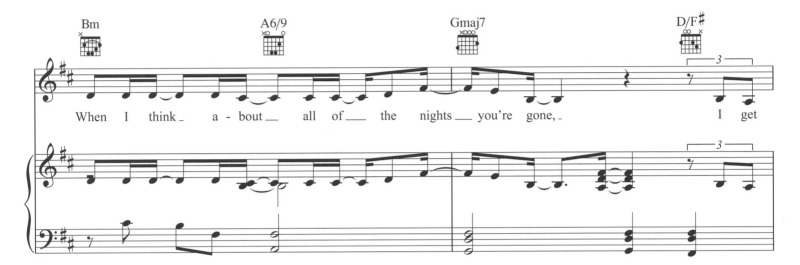

53

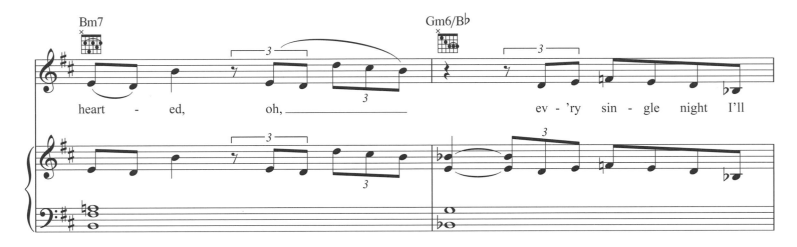

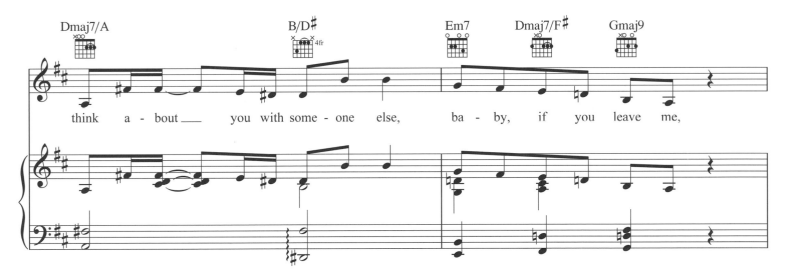

54

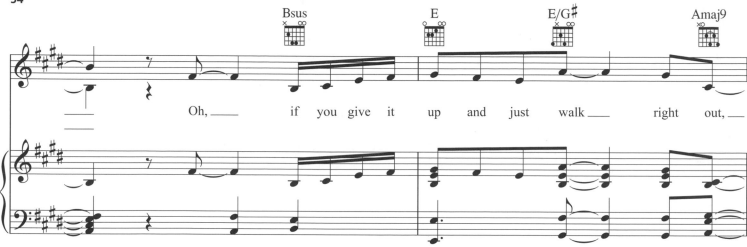

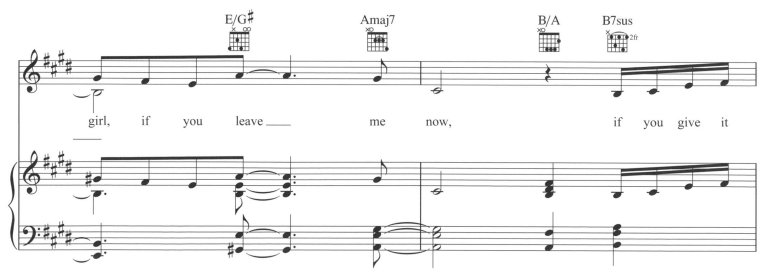

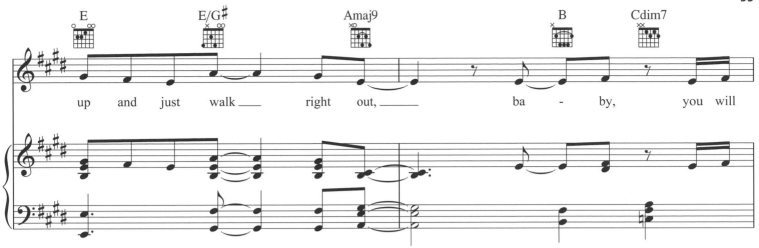

up and just walk ___ right out, _____ ba - by, you will

take the big - gest part ___ of me ___ and all the things ___ that I ___ be - lieve, ___

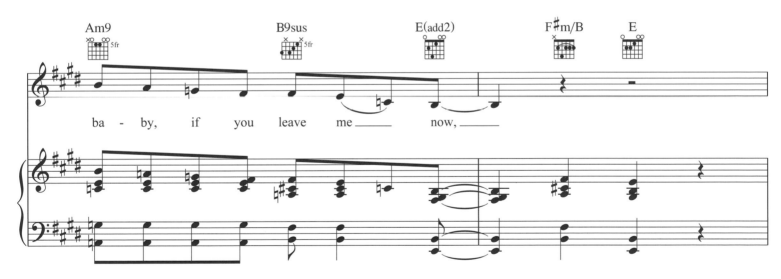

ba - by, if you leave me _____ now, _____

ba - by, if you leave me now, ___ oh, oh, oh, oh.

SLOW IT DOWN

Words and Music by CHARLIE PUTH,
JACOB KASHER HINDLIN, RAMI RACOUB,
DARYL HALL, JOHN OATES,
SARA ALLEN and CARL FALK

I got a sit-u-a-tion, this girl been stress-in' me.
She knows just what she do-in', she fuck-in' with my head.

Say-in' she bet-ter be the on-ly___ one.___ My life is com-pli-cat-ed,
Wrap-pin' her legs so tight a-round my___ waist.___ Two in the af-ter-noon but

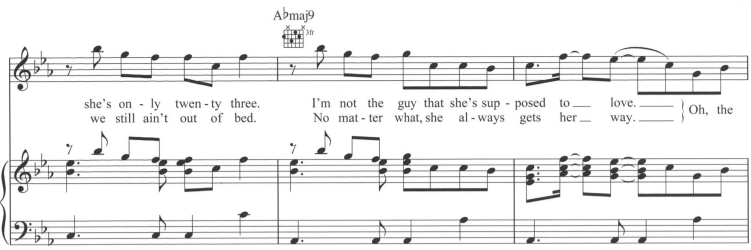

she's on - ly twen - ty three. I'm not the guy that she's sup - posed to _ love. _ }Oh, the
we still ain't out of bed. No mat - ter what, she al - ways gets her _ way. _

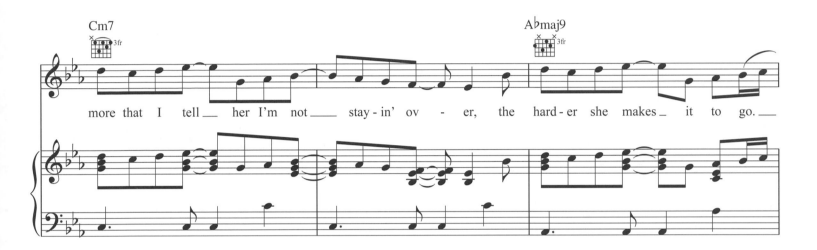

more that I tell _ her I'm not _ stay - in' ov - er, the hard - er she makes _ it to go. _

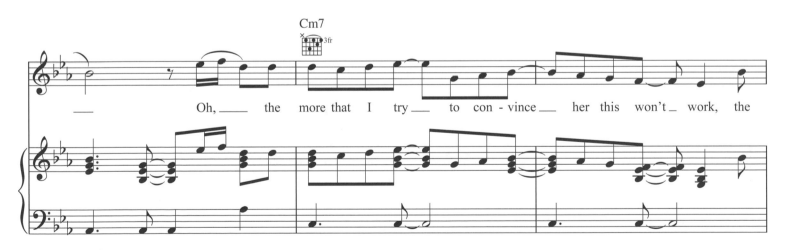

_ Oh, _ the more that I try _ to con - vince _ her this won't _ work, the

fast - er she takes _ off her clothes. _ Girl, you got - ta slow it down. _

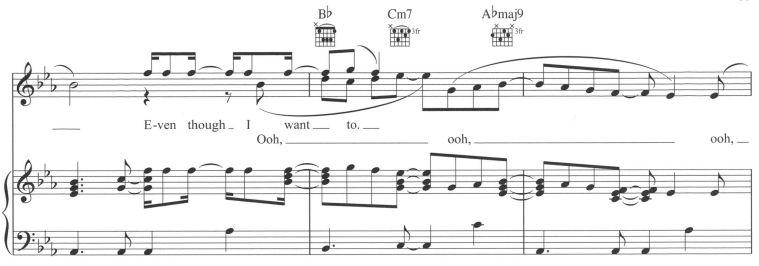

E-ven though ___ I want ___ to. ___
Ooh, _____ ooh, _____ ooh, ___

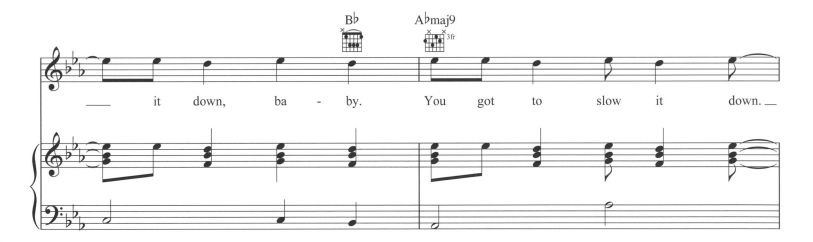

You got to slow it, slow ___

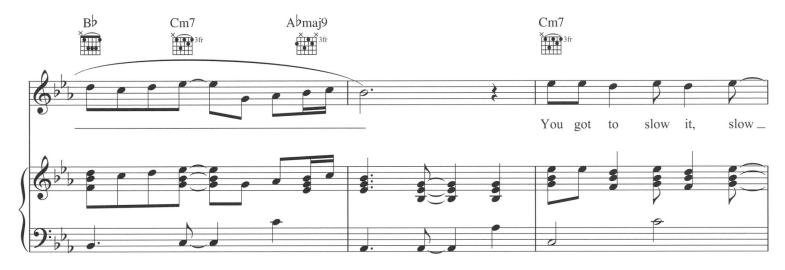

___ it down, ba - by. You got to slow it down. ___

___ You don't know what you're do - in' to me now. You got to slow it, slow ___

it down, ba - by. You got to slow it down. _____ Girl, you got - ta

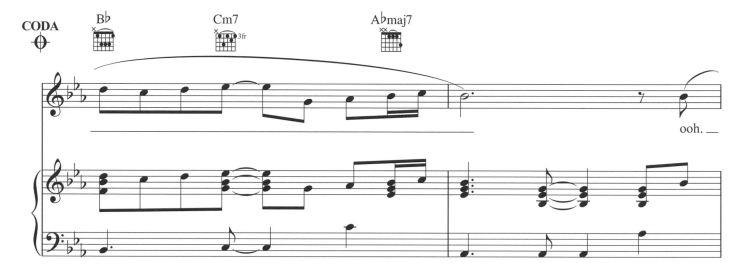

CODA

ooh. _____

Ooh, _____ ooh. ___

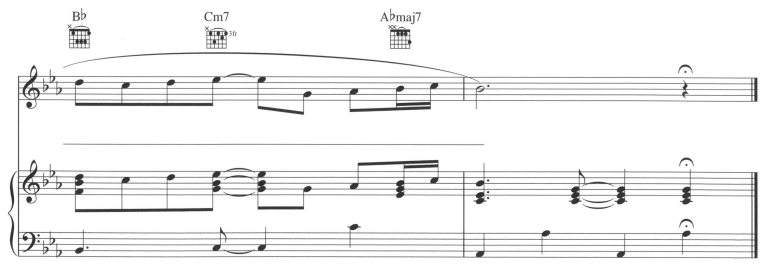

CHANGE

Words and Music by CHARLIE PUTH,
JENS CARLSSON and ROSS GOLAN

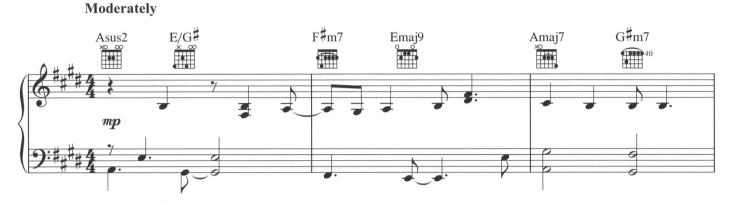

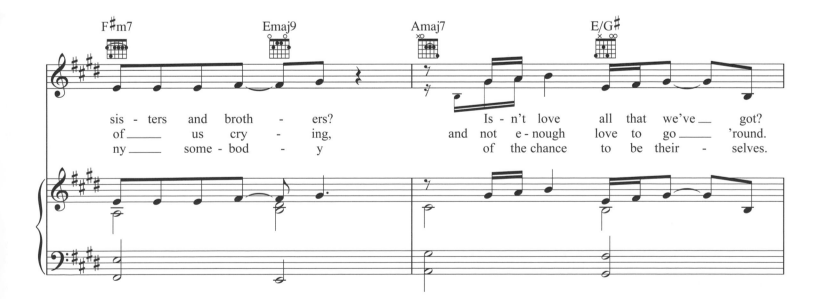

So we know ev - 'ry-one's got a
What a waste; an - oth-er day, an - oth - er
What a waste it would be if we

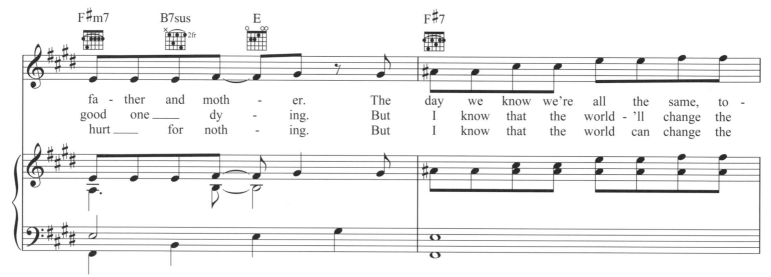

fa - ther and moth - er. The day we know we're all the same, to -
good one ___ dy - ing. But I know that the world - 'll change the
hurt ___ for noth - ing. But I know that the world can change the

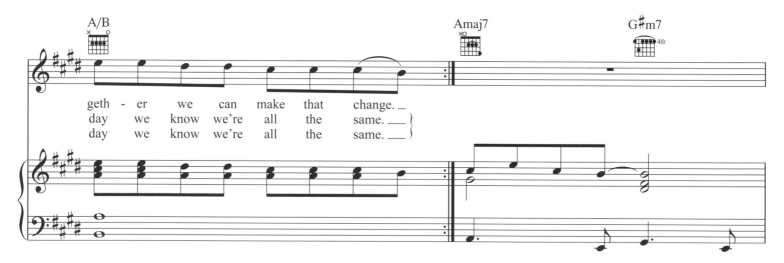

geth - er we can make that change. ___
day we know we're all the same. ___ }
day we know we're all the same. ___ }

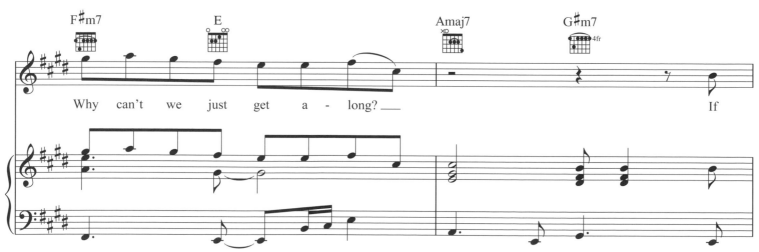

Why can't we just get a - long? ___ If

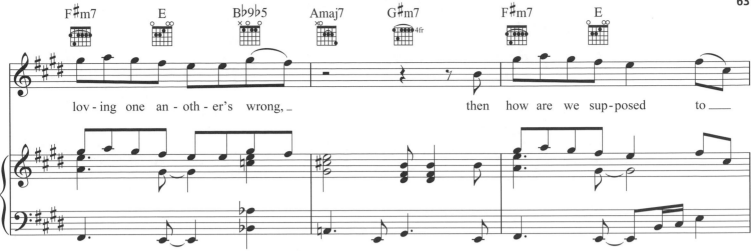

lov-ing one an-oth-er's wrong, _____ then how are we sup-posed to ____

To Coda $\oplus$

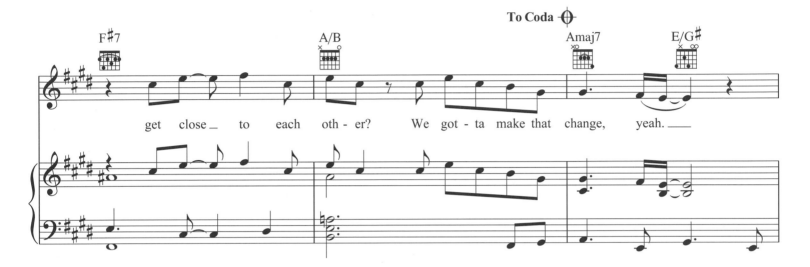

get close _ to each oth-er? We got-ta make that change, yeah. ____

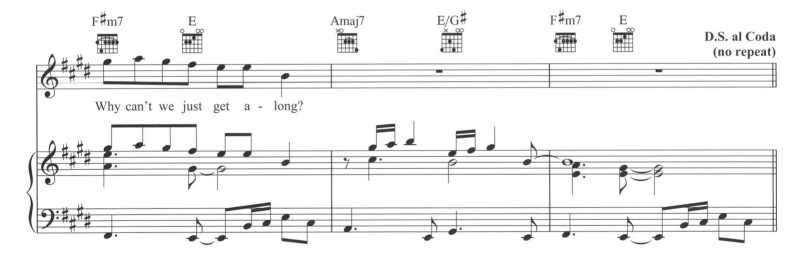

Why can't we just get a - long?

D.S. al Coda (no repeat)

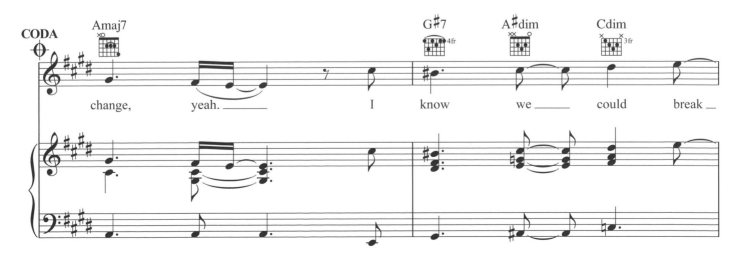

CODA $\oplus$

change, yeah. _____ I know we ____ could break ____

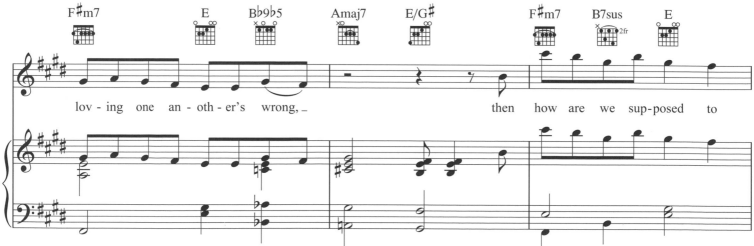

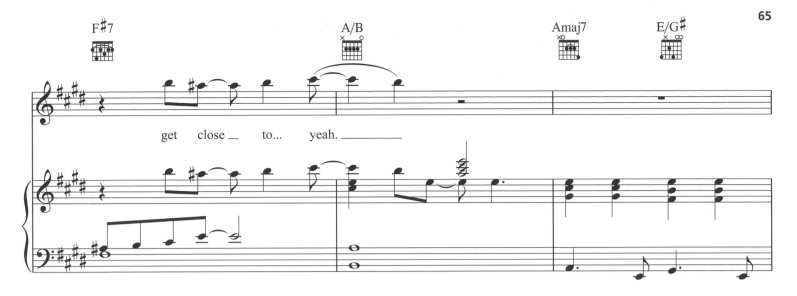

get close __ to... yeah. ___

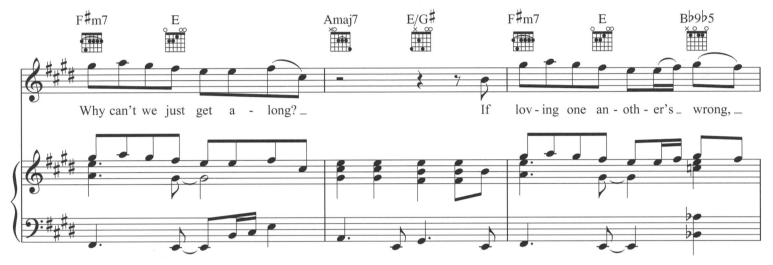

Why can't we just get a - long? _ If lov-ing one an-oth-er's _ wrong, _

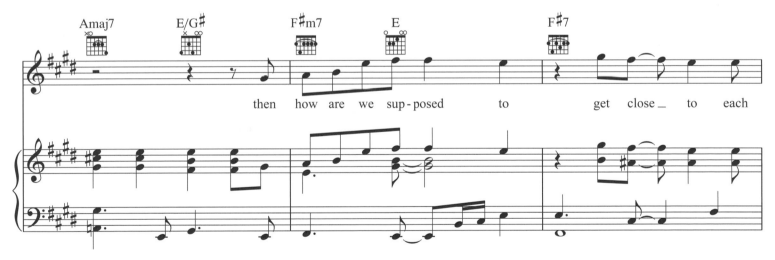

then how are we sup-posed to get close __ to each

oth-er? We got - ta make that change, yeah, ___ that change, yeah. _

molto rit.

SOMEBODY TOLD ME

Words and Music by CHARLIE PUTH,
JACOB KASHER HINDLIN
and JENS CARLSSON

With energy

I was just ___ with you ___ on your birth - day ___ and I met ___
___ but ask, ___ "Who is that, ___ babe?" And the way ___

___ your whole ___ fam - i - ly. ___ But on the way ___ home, ___
___ you said, ___ "No - bod - y." ___ I knew the ru - ___ mors, ___

___ you kept look - ing at your ___ phone. ___ Could - n't help ___
___ they were more than just ru - ___

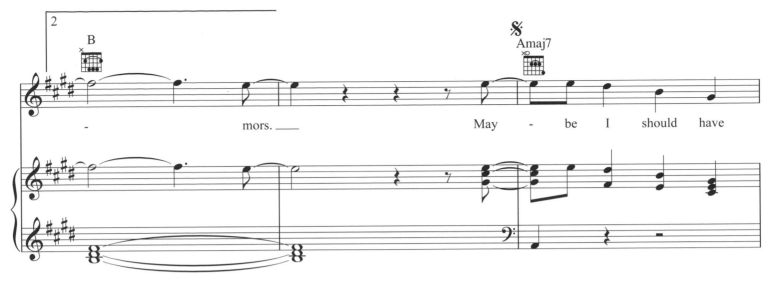

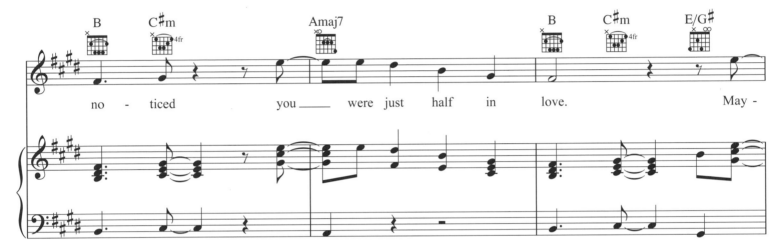

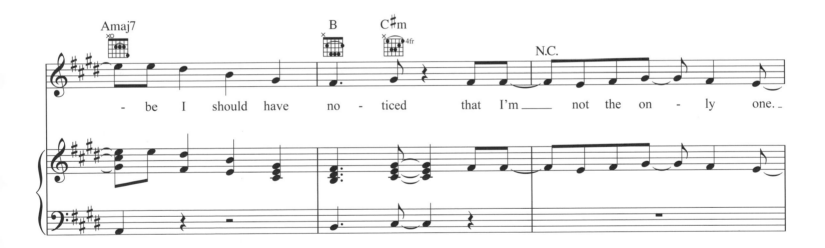

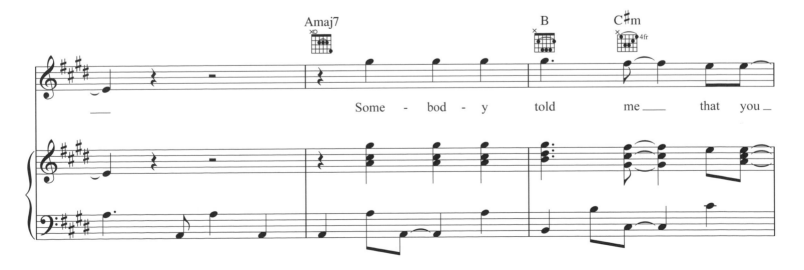

got an-oth-er lov-er you've been giv-ing it to.____ Can't be-lieve

I be-lieved you,____ you____ were my _____ girl.__

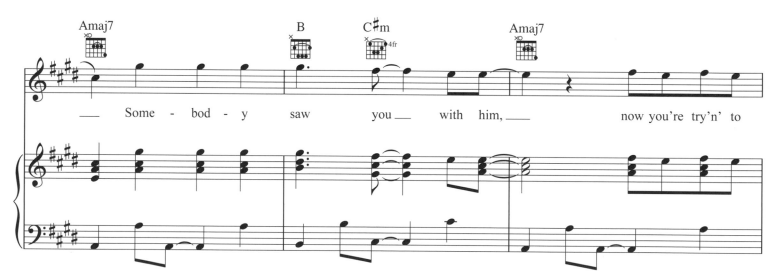

__ Some-bod-y saw you__ with him,___ now you're try'n' to

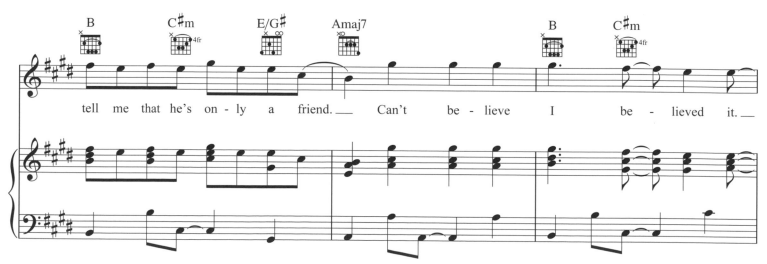

tell me that he's on-ly a friend.___ Can't be-lieve I be-lieved it.__

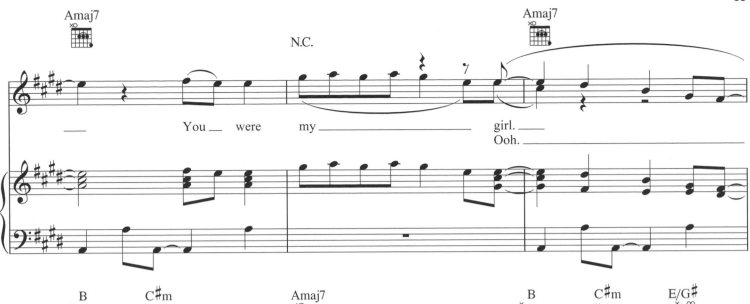

You ___ were ___ my _____ girl. ___
Ooh. _____

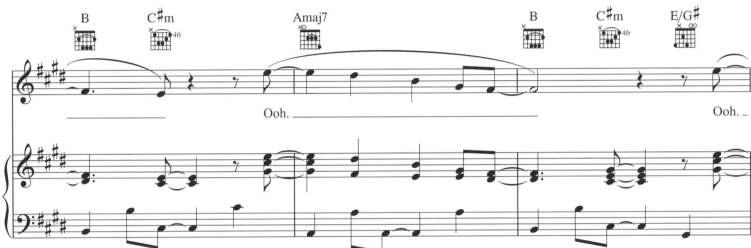

Ooh. _____ Ooh. _

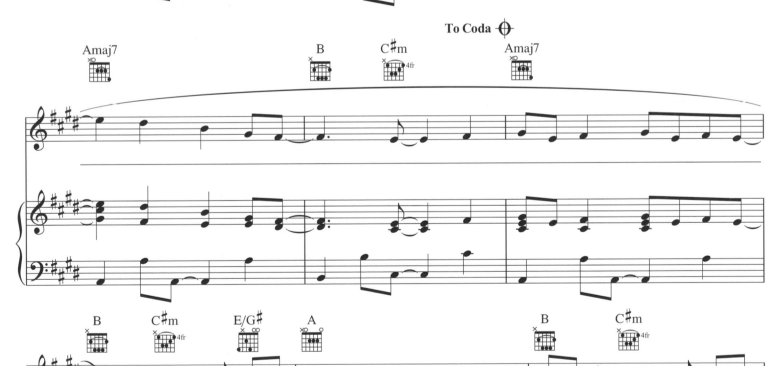

To Coda ⊕

Late - ly you've ___ been mak - ing ex - cus - es and the sto -

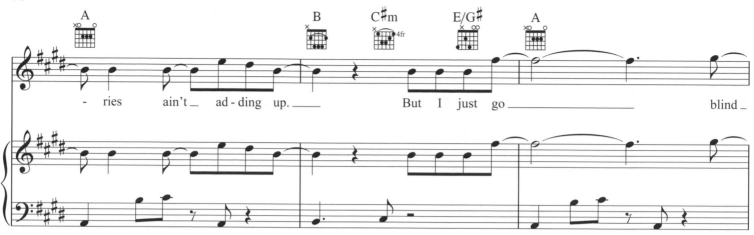

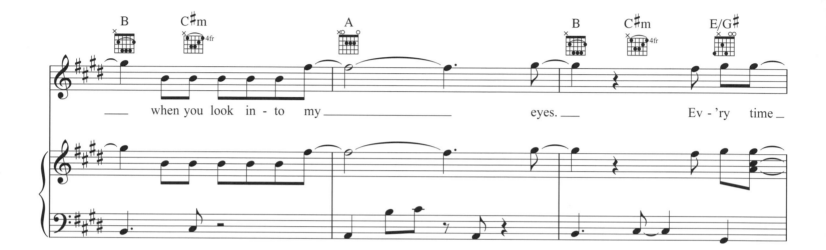

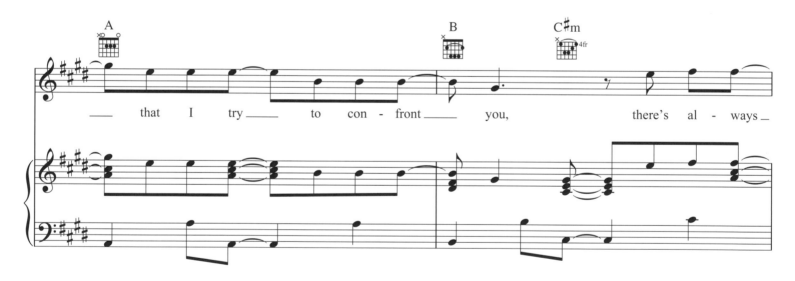

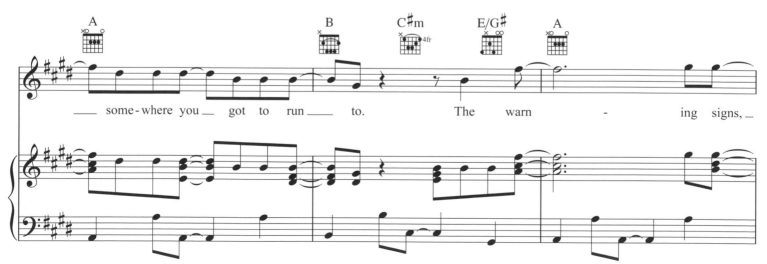

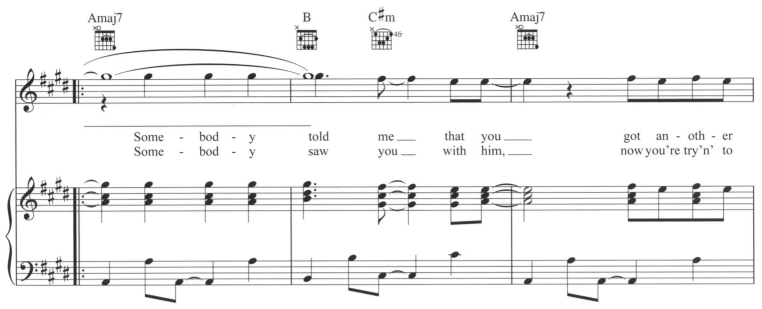

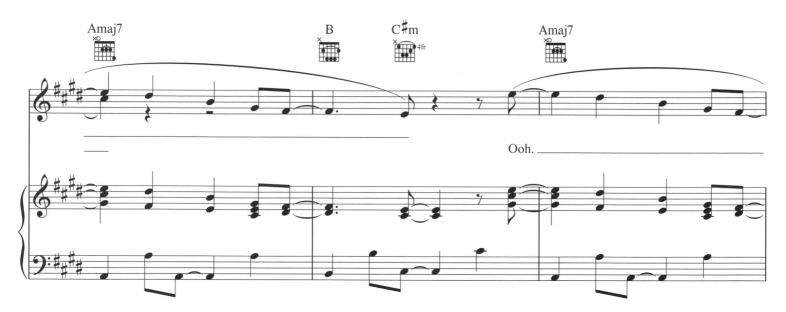

Ooh.

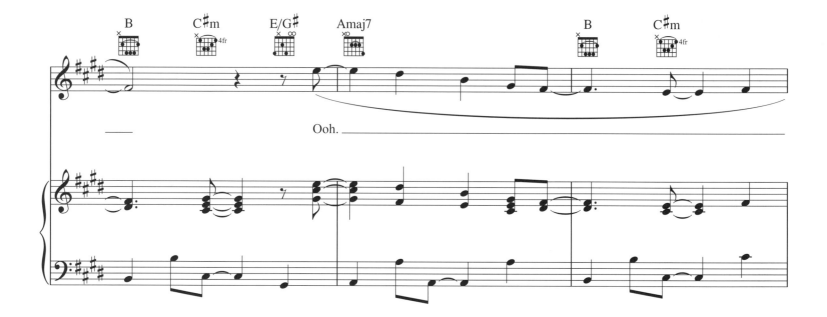

Ooh.

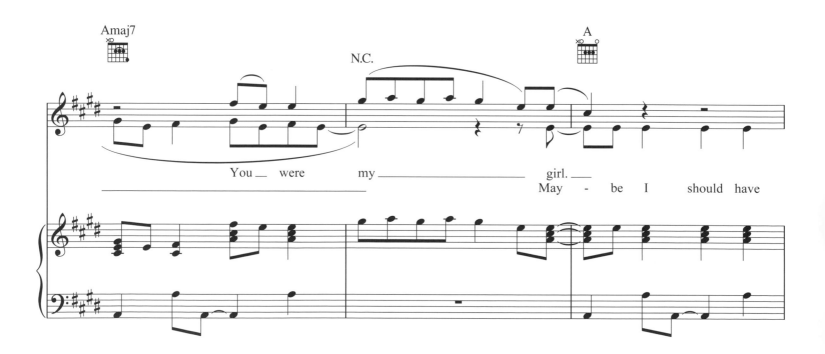

You _ were my _____ girl. __

May - be I should have

THROUGH IT ALL

Words and Music by CHARLIE PUTH,
JACOB KASHER HINDLIN
and BREYAN ISAAC

Gospel Ballad

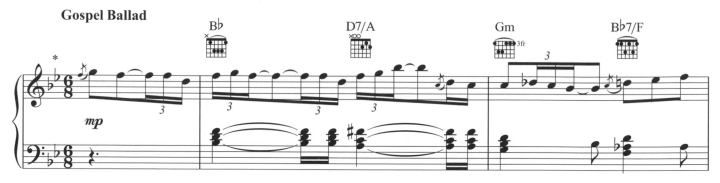

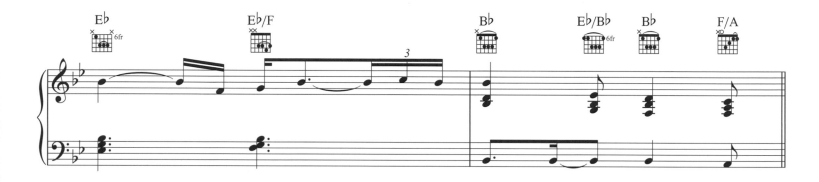

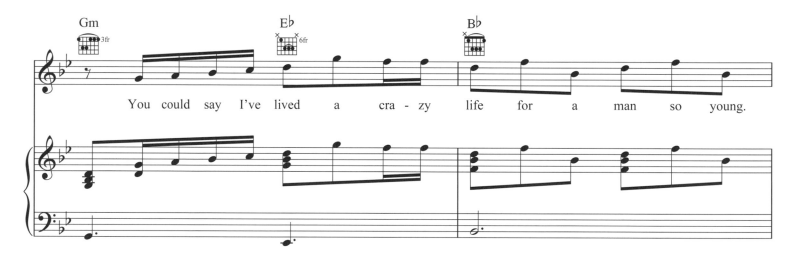

You could say I've lived a cra-zy life for a man so young.

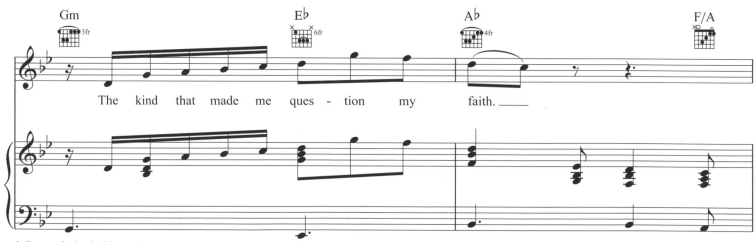

The kind that made me ques-tion my faith. _____

* *Recorded a half step lower.*

Now I'm look-ing back just won-der-ing where the time has gone,

but I guess it's just the price you ___ pay. ___

I've al-read-y loved more than I thought I could love some-one.
Grow-ing up in this wild cit-y, you had to fight or run.

I've al-read-y felt my heart break. ___
Now you know why I'm not a-fraid. ___

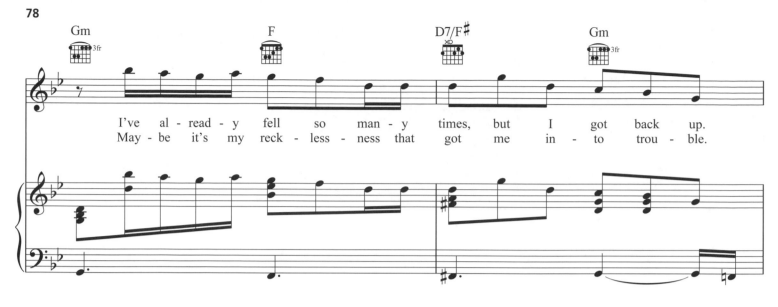

I've al-read-y fell so man-y times, but I got back up.
May-be it's my reck-less-ness that got me in-to trou-ble.

But at least I did it all my way. _____ I've been ____ through it
But at least I did it all my way. _____

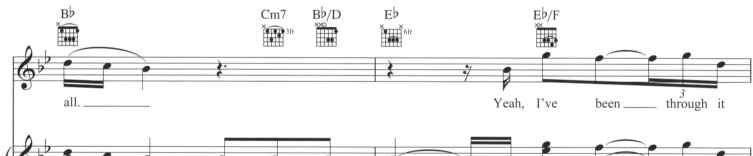

all. _____ Yeah, I've been ____ through it

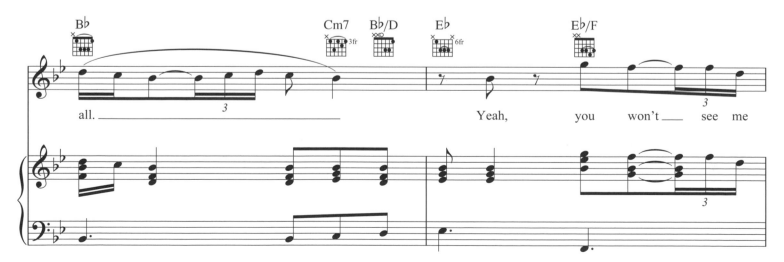

all. _____ Yeah, you won't ___ see me

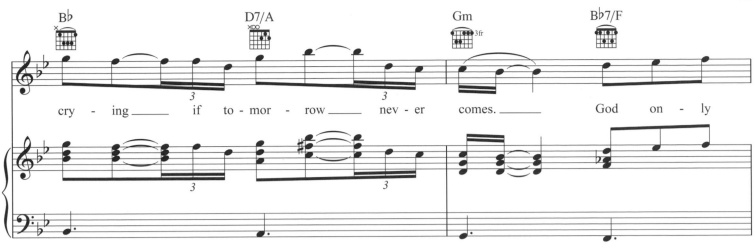

cry - ing ____ if to - mor - row ____ nev - er comes. ____ God on - ly

knows, ___ I've been ____ through it all. ____

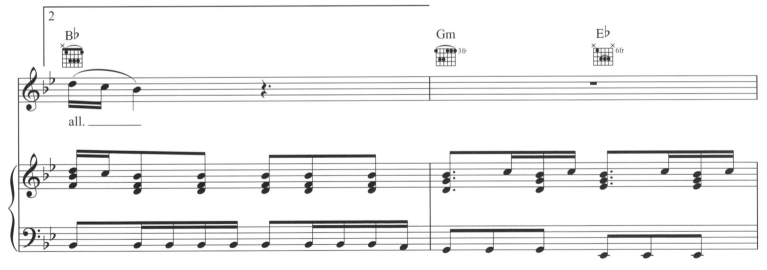

all. ____

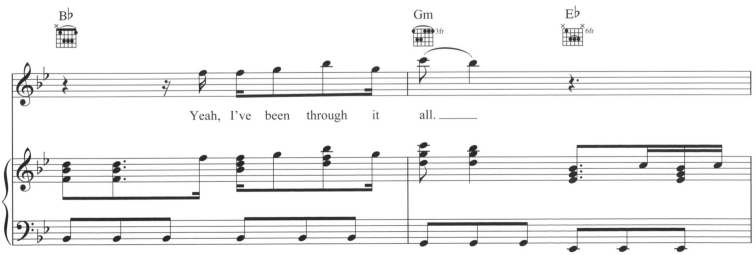

Yeah, I've been through it all. ____

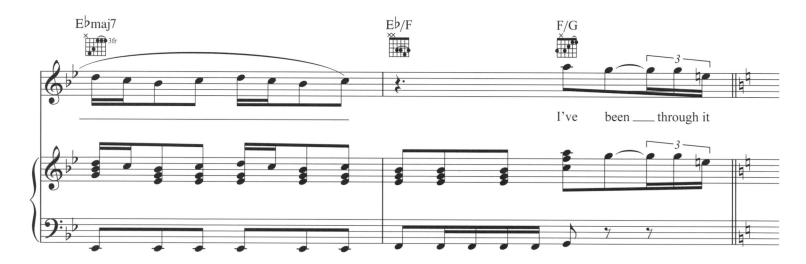

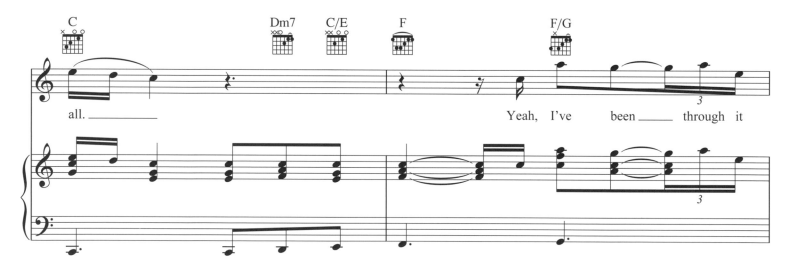

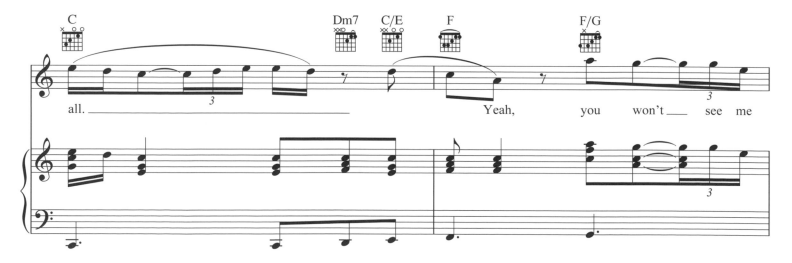

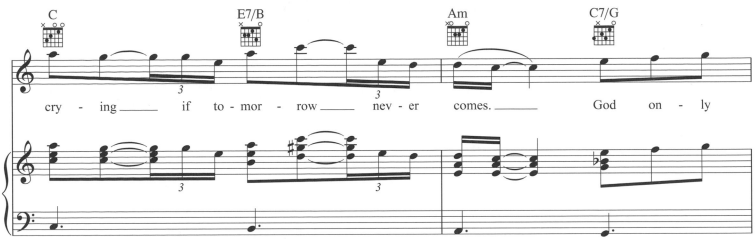

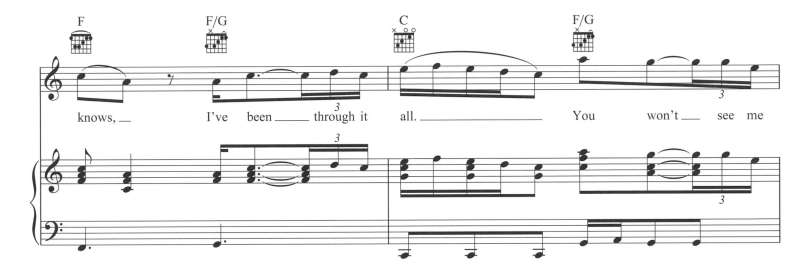

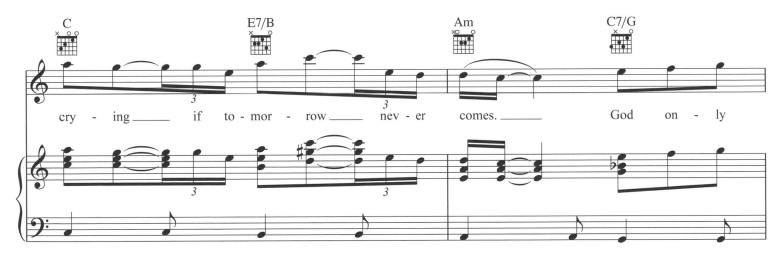

EMPTY CUPS

Words and Music by CHARLIE PUTH,
JACOB KASHER HINDLIN, JAMES GHALEB,
RICHARD GORANSSON and SAVAN KOTECHA

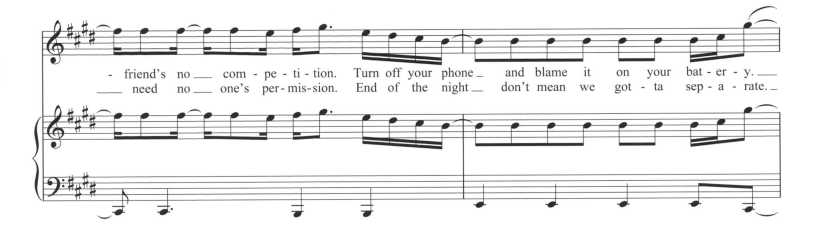

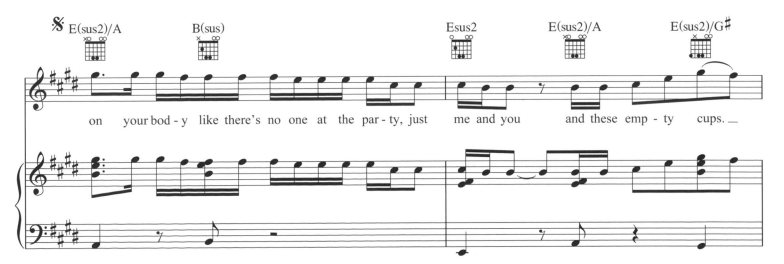

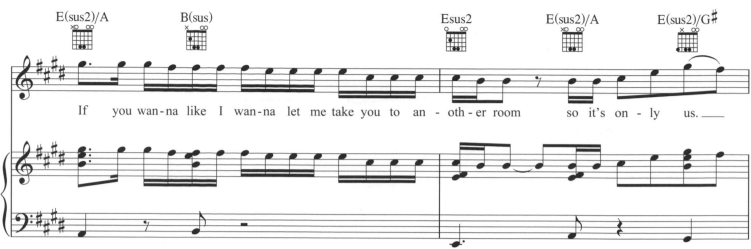

If you wan-na like I wan-na let me take you to an - oth-er room so it's on-ly us. __

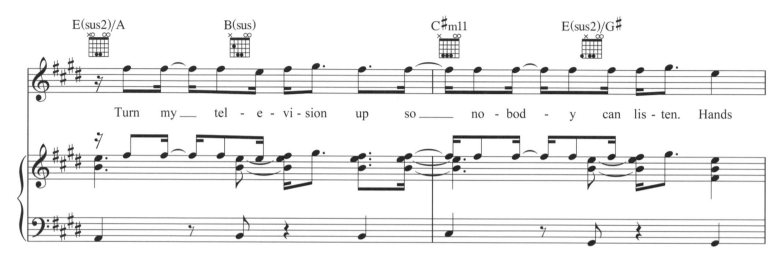

Turn my __ tel - e - vi - sion up so __ no - bod - y can lis - ten. Hands

To Coda ⊕

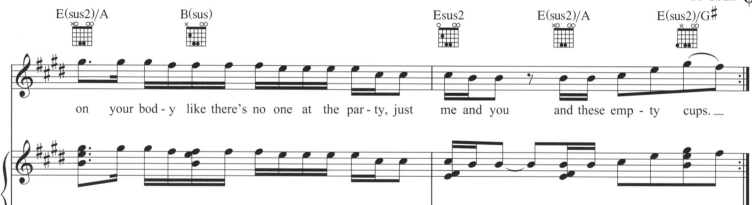

on your bod - y like there's no one at the par - ty, just me and you and these emp - ty cups. __

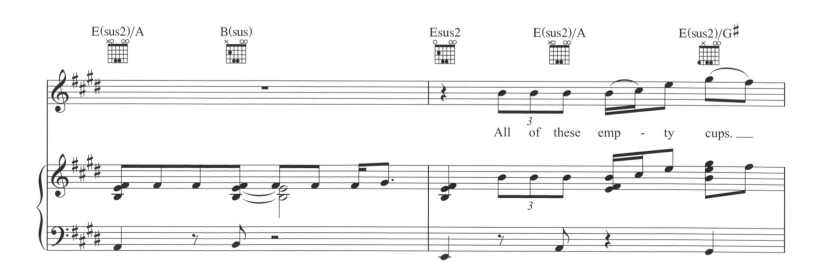

All of these emp - ty cups. __

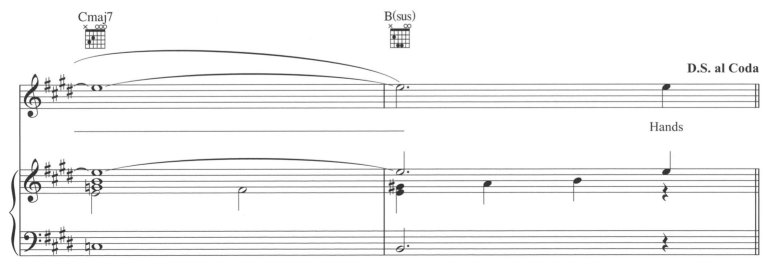

MORE FROM YOUR FAVORITE ARTISTS

CAMILA CABELLO – CAMILA

All ten tracks from the 2018 debut album by this Fifth Harmony alum which debuted at the top of the Billboard® 200 album charts. Our folio includes piano/vocal/guitar arrangements for the hit single "Havana" plus: All These Years • Consequences • In the Dark • Inside Out • Into It • Never Be the Same • Real Friends • She Loves Control • Something's Gotta Give.
00268761 P/V/G $17.99

ARIANA GRANDE – MY EVERYTHING

This sophomore solo effort from the Nickelodeon TV star turned R&B songstress reached #1 on the Billboard® 200 album charts and has produced several popular hits. A dozen tracks are featured in piano/vocal/guitar arrangements: Be My Baby • Best Mistake • Break Free • Break Your Heart Right Back • Hands on Me • Intro • Just a Little Bit of Your Heart • Love Me Harder • My Everything • One Last Time • Problem • Why Try.
00146042 P/V/G $17.99

NIALL HORAN – FLICKER

This debut solo effort from One Direction's Niall Horan debuted at the top of the Billboard® 200 album charts. Our piano/vocal/guitar folio includes 13 songs from the album: Fire Away • Flicker • Mirrors • On My Own • On the Loose • Paper Houses • Seeing Blind • Since We're Alone • Slow Hands • This Town • The Tide • Too Much to Ask • You and Me.
00255614 P/V/G $17.99

IMAGINE DRAGONS – EVOLVE

This 3rd studio album by Nevada rock band Imagine Dragons was released in the summer of 2017 and reached #2 on the Billboard® 200 album charts. Our matching folio includes piano, vocal & guitar arrangements to the singles "Believer" and "Thunder" as well as 9 moresongs: Dancing in the Dark • I Don't Know Why • I'll Make It Up to You • Mouth of the River • Rise Up • Start Over • Walking the Wire • Whatever It Takes • Yesterday.
00243903 P/V/G $17.99

MAROON 5 – RED PILL BLUES

Maroon 5 keeps churning out the hits with their sixth studio album, this 2017 release led by the single "What Lovers Do" featuring Sza. Our songbooks features piano/vocal/guitar arrangements of this song and 14 more: Best 4 U • Bet My Heart • Closure • Cold • Denim Jacket • Don't Wanna Know • Girls like You • Help Me Out • Lips on You • Plastic Rose • Visions • Wait • Whiskey • Who I Am.
00261247 P/V/G $17.99

P!NK – BEAUTIFUL TRAUMA

This 7th studio album from pop superstar Pink topped the Billboard® 200 album charts upon its release in 2017 led by the single "What About Us." Our matching folio features this song and a dozen more for piano, voice and guitar: Barbies • Beautiful Trauma • Better Life • But We Lost It • For Now • I Am Here • Revenge • Secrets • Whatever You Want • Where We Go • Wild Hearts Can't Be Broken • You Get My Love.
00255621 P/V/G $17.99

ED SHEERAN – DIVIDE

This third studio album release from Ed Sheeran topped the Billboard® 200 album charts upon its March 2017 release, led by the singles "Castle on the Hill" and "Shape of You." Our matching folio includes these two hits, plus 14 others: Barcelona • Dive • Eraser • Galway Girl • Hearts Don't Break Around Here • New Man • Perfect • Save Myself • What Do I Know? • and more.
00233553 P/V/G $17.99

SAM SMITH – THE THRILL OF IT ALL

Smith's sophomore album release in 2017 topped the Billboard® 200 album charts. This matching folio features 14 songs: Baby, You Make Me Crazy • Burning • Him • Midnight Train • No Peace • Nothing Left for You • One Day at a Time • One Last Song • Palace • Pray • Say It First • Scars • The Thrill of It All • Too Good at Goodbyes.
00257746 P/V/G $19.99

TAYLOR SWIFT – REPUTATION

Taylor's 2017 album release continues her chart-topping success, debuting on the Billboard® 200 chart at number 1, led by the first singles "Look What You Made Me Do" and "...Ready for It." Our songbook features these 2 songs plus 13 more arranged for piano and voice with guitar chord frames: Call It What You Want • Dancing with Our Hands Tied • Delicate • Don't Blame Me • Dress • End Game • Getaway Car • Gorgeous • I Did Something Bad • King of My Heart • New Year's Day • So It Goes... • This Is Why We Can't Have Nice Things.
00262694 P/V/G $17.99